TRIED IN THE FURNACE

My Journey from Pain to Purpose

Keisha Sheppard

COPYRIGHT PAGE

Tried in the Furnace: My Journey from Pain to Purpose © 2026 by **Keisha Sheppard**

All rights reserved.

No part of this book may be reproduced, distributed, or transmitted in any form or by any means—electronic, mechanical, photocopying, recording, or otherwise—without the prior written permission of the author, except in the case of brief quotations used in reviews or scholarly works.

This book is a work of nonfiction. Some names and identifying details have been changed to protect the privacy of individuals.

Scripture quotations are taken from the Holy Bible, King James Version (KJV).

Printed in the United States of America.

First Edition

DEDICATION

To my husband, Taj. Baby, I love you. I've loved you since we were kids. I would walk through the shadows of death again if I had to, just to bring you out. Your love, patience, and unwavering support have carried me through storms I never thought I would survive. Thank you for being my anchor, my joy, and my safe place.

To my children, Keshawn, Keshae, Greg, and Rashad, thank you for growing up with me and standing beside me through every trial, every failure, and every moment of pain. You have made me stronger, wiser, and more resilient than I ever imagined. Together, we survived, we thrived, and we built a family rooted in love, faith, and perseverance.

To my young grandchildren, Kali, Kartier, and Kenzie, this book is my blueprint for you. It is a guide to surviving life's storms by calling on Jesus, finding your faith, and knowing that even in the darkest moments, hope is possible.

To my mother. Mom, I'm sorry for my rebellious and disrespectful attitude at times. Please know it was not aimed at you, but was a reaction to pain too heavy for a young girl to bear. I love you and appreciate every sacrifice, every lesson, and every moment of love you gave despite life's hardships.

To my deceased father. Dad, your love shaped my heart. Though I feared losing you to your own struggles, God allowed you to live until sixty-nine, giving me memories, guidance, and the blessing of knowing your spirit. Your life, your journey, and your love have impacted mine in ways I will carry forever.

This book is never meant to expose family secrets or to hurt anyone. It is meant to grow, heal, and inspire.

CONTENT

DEDICATION	iii
CONTENT	iv
PREFACE	1
INTRODUCTION	2
CHAPTER 1	3
Innocence Interrupted	*3*
CHAPTER 2	5
The Night My Innocence Was Stolen	*5*
Chapter 3	7
Carrying Secrets, Learning to Survive	*7*
CHAPTER 4	9
The Weight of Silence	*9*
Chapter 5	11
Running Away and Learning How to Survive	*11*
CHAPTER 6	13
Rebellion and the Need to Escape	*13*
CHAPTER 7	14
Motherhood and Independence	*14*
Chapter 8	16
The Day I Set My Soul Free	*16*
CHAPTER 9	17
Struggle, Survival, and Seeds of Faith	*17*

CHAPTER 10 — 18
The Dream of Forgiveness — 18

CHAPTER 11 — 21
When Love Turns to Ashes — 21

CHAPTER 12 — 25
Reflection and Grace — 25

CHAPTER 13 — 27
From Grief to Awakening — 27

CHAPTER 14 — 29
Healing, Forgiveness, and Restoration — 29

CHAPTER 15 — 30
Trials and Divine Protection — 30

CHAPTER 16 — 32
The Visitation — 32

CHAPTER 17 — 34
The Dream of the Man in White — 34

Chapter 18 — 36
Living Fully, Loving Deeply — 36

Chapter 19 — 38
Healing and Reflecting — 38

CHAPTER 20 — 40
Freedom, Family, and Purpose — 40

CHAPTER 21 — 42
The Day the Mirror Didn't Smile — 42

CHAPTER 22	**44**
A Dream of the Narrow Way	*44*
CHAPTER 23	**46**
The House, the Glowing Wood, and the Keys	*46*
Chapter 24	**49**
When Death Spoke, God Answered	*49*
CHAPTER 25	**52**
After the Miracle	*52*
Scripture Index	**55**
A Blessing From My Heart to Yours	*56*
About the Author	**59**

My Journey from Pain to Purpose

PREFACE

Life doesn't come with warnings. It doesn't tell you when the pain will arrive, when the people you trust will let you down, or when the world will challenge every ounce of your courage. *Tried in the Furnace* is my story, a story of pain, of survival, and ultimately, of hope.

I have walked through moments that threatened to break me. Moments of fear, of loss, and of uncertainty that felt heavier than I could bear. I have held my children in my arms, wondering how I would protect them from a world that seemed determined to test us. I have faced betrayal, danger, and the kind of heartbreak that leaves scars you can't always see.

But through it all, I learned something powerful. Even in the fire, even in the darkest nights, we can endure. We can rise. We can choose faith over fear, love over anger, and hope over despair.

This book is my journey, unfiltered, raw, and honest. It is a testament to resilience, to the strength of a mother's love, to the power of family, and to the grace of God that carried me through every storm. I share it because I want anyone who feels lost, overwhelmed, or broken to know this. You are not alone, and your story is not over. There is hope. There is light. There is a way forward.

I invite you to walk with me through my life, to feel the fear, the sorrow, and the pain, but also the triumph, the joy, and the unshakable faith that grew from it all. This is my truth. My testimony. My heart laid bare.

With love, courage, and faith,

Keisha Sheppard

INTRODUCTION

This is my story, and I would not change it if I could. Every trauma, pain, loss, and rejection has been a lesson that built within me the fruits of the Spirit: meekness, long-suffering, endurance, strength, love, mercy, grace, repentance, and forgiveness.

I am releasing this book because I have accomplished what the Lord sent me here to receive. Now, I release it back into the world as my testimony of His goodness throughout my trials and tribulations.

I am at peace with my family, friends, and the world, without regret, having learned the lessons that lead me to Jesus for all of eternity.

CHAPTER 1

Innocence Interrupted

From the moment I took my first breath on January 4, 1978, life demanded that I fight. I was born sickly, a fragile thread of life in a world that offered no guarantees. Doctors said it was unlikely I would survive. Two other infants born on the same day had already died from the same condition, a diaphragmatic hernia. My tiny body fought with every heartbeat, and my cries were my first prayers.

But it was not just my strength keeping me alive. My grandmother, my parents, and countless family members lifted their voices in prayer, calling on Jesus to hold me close, to spare my life, and to set a plan in motion that I would not understand until decades later.

Even as a baby, I was wrapped in faith. Every whispered, "Lord, protect her," felt like a shield around me, though I would not comprehend the magnitude of it until years later. And somehow, against the odds, I survived.

I grew up in my father's mother's house in Washington, D.C., surrounded by family. My sisters, Mia and Monique, and my brothers, Montae and Gregory Jr., whom we called Lil' Greg, were my constant companions. Life was not perfect. My parents did not get along. My father battled drug addiction, and the air in the house often vibrated with tension. Yet, amidst that tension were small pockets of love, laughter, and safety that made childhood bearable.

When I was nine, my parents separated, and my mother moved us to Sheriff Road in the Lodge Apartments. It was a new chapter, full of uncertainty but also moments of happiness. It was there, in the fourth grade, that I met Taj, a boy who would later become the love of my life. At the time, he was just a neighborhood friend, someone whose smile made the world feel a little lighter.

Shortly after moving, my mother met Mark and eventually married him. He brought two children into the family, Dave and Marie, but to me and my younger sister, Mia, he was fun, loving, and full of life. Mark made ordinary moments feel magical. Late night store runs for snacks. Movies and the Discovery Channel. Laughter that left our stomachs hurting. Christmases filled with gifts and warmth.

For a while, it felt like we had finally found our rhythm.

Through it all, I carried a quiet sense that God had a plan. Even in chaos, even in struggle, there was a thread of purpose running through my life, a promise that my story was far from over.

But innocence is fragile.

And mine was about to be shattered.

Pain often arrives without warning. One moment, life feels familiar, and the next, everything you trusted begins to shake. The furnace does not ask permission before it ignites. It simply reveals what must be refined.

This chapter marks the moment when the fire was no longer avoidable.

Scripture

Isaiah 43:2 (KJV) *When thou passest through the waters, I will be with thee; and through the rivers, they shall not overflow thee: when thou walkest through the fire, thou shalt not be burned; neither shall the flame kindle upon thee.*

Prayer

Lord, I did not ask for this fire, but I trust You in it. If this is the place where You refine me, then stay close. Do not let the flames consume me. Let them transform me.

Amen.

CHAPTER 2

The Night My Innocence Was Stolen

Growing up, Mark seemed like the kind of person who could make anything fun. He joked with me and my sister, Mia, took us on late night snack runs, and made us feel seen and included. In those moments, I felt safe. I thought this was how family was supposed to feel.

But one night, everything changed.

I was in third grade. That day, I had worked hard selling items for a school fundraiser. The grand prize was a Super Nintendo. I sold one hundred items, not enough to win, but enough to feel proud. That night, I went to bed in my long pink Strawberry Shortcake nightgown, tired but happy. Mia slept on the top bunk. I slept on the bottom.

I do not know how long I had been asleep when I felt it, hands touching me.

My eyes flew open, and there he was, sitting at the foot of my bed. The man who made me laugh. The man who brought Christmas joy. My body froze. My mind screamed for my mother, for anyone, but no one came.

When I stirred, he pulled his hands away, eyes wide and bloodshot, nervous and afraid I would tell. He left the room, but the tears did not stop. I felt confused, violated, and alone.

Shortly after, he returned. He placed money under my pillow and warned me that if I told, my mother would not believe me or like me anymore.

That night, innocence slipped through my fingers. Fear and betrayal took its place.

The next morning, I ran to my cousin Bree's apartment across the hall and told her everything. She told me not to tell my father, warning that he might hurt Mark if he found out. So I stayed silent.

Even then, I prayed. Quietly. Desperately.

"Jesus, please do not let him hurt me again."

Somehow, even in the darkness, God's hand was still there, holding me, protecting me, carrying me forward.

But a part of me hardened that night.

And childhood was never the same.

Some nights divide a life into before and after. This was not just the loss of safety. It was the theft of innocence, trust, and the freedom to remain a child.

What happened that night was not your fault.

You did not invite it.

You did not deserve it.

I constantly told myself.

The fire began here, but so did God's quiet keeping of my soul, even when I did not yet know His name.

Scripture

Psalm 34:18 (KJV) *"The Lord is close to the brokenhearted and saves those who are crushed in spirit."*

Prayer

Lord Jesus, You saw me that night, the child who did not have words, protection, or understanding. You saw what was taken, and You did not look away.

I place that child into Your hands now. Cover her with what she should have had. Heal what was violated. Restore what was stolen.

Where innocence was taken, plant peace.

Where silence was forced, release truth.

Where shame tried to live, let Your love remain.

Amen.

Chapter 3

Carrying Secrets, Learning to Survive

After that night, life continued, but I had changed.

The house no longer felt safe. Mark was still there, still laughing, still pretending nothing had happened. I carried the secret like a stone in my chest. I did not tell my father. I did not tell my mother. Fear silenced me.

Every night, I prayed quietly. "Lord, please protect me. Help me survive."

My siblings became my anchor. Laughter still existed, but beneath it lived fear and confusion. I could not understand how the same man could bring both joy and destruction.

When I was twelve, tragedy struck again. My brother, Lil' Greg, was killed in a senseless accident, a stray bullet from a gun meant for play. He and his friends got hold of a gun, and he accidentally shot himself. For twenty years, I carried guilt, convinced I had failed him.

After his death, my relationship with my mother and siblings fractured. We were all grieving, but in different ways. Arguments became constant. Home felt like a battlefield.

By sixteen, I turned to weed to numb the pain. It became survival, a way to escape grief, fear, and anger. I rebelled, lashed out, and searched for relief anywhere I could find it.

Through it all, I prayed. Even when faith felt fragile, it never disappeared.

I was learning how to survive, unaware that this survival would one day become testimony.

Some burdens are invisible. They do not bruise the skin, but they bend the spine of the soul. Carrying secrets teaches a child how to survive through silence. You learn how to smile while holding pain. How to protect everyone else while disappearing inside yourself.

The secret was not just what happened. The secret was having to live as if it did not matter.

Scripture

Psalm 56:8"(KJV) Thou tellest my wanderings*: put thou my tears into thy bottle: are they not in thy book?*

Prayer

God, I carried what was too heavy for my age. I learned to lock pain away because no one told me it was safe to speak.

You saw the nights I cried quietly. You heard the questions I never asked out loud. You stayed near when silence felt like the only protection I had.

I release the burden of secrecy now. What I hid to survive, I place in Your hands to heal. Teach me that my voice is not dangerous. It is necessary.

Amen.

CHAPTER 4

The Weight of Silence

Silence became both my shield and my prison.

I learned early that speaking the truth came with consequences — disbelief, shame, confusion. So I stayed quiet. I smiled. I helped others. I pretended I was fine.

But silence suffocates the soul.

Nights were the hardest. I lay awake replaying moments, wishing someone would ask if I was okay. But I had learned that silence felt safer than rejection.

For years, I mistook silence for strength.

Until one day, the weight became unbearable.

I cried out to God, not in whispers, but in surrender. And peace came. Not because the past disappeared, but because I finally released it.

Psalm 34:17–18 became my lifeline:

"The Lord is close to the brokenhearted and saves those who are crushed in spirit."

Silence can feel like protection at first. It promises safety. It keeps the peace. It avoids questions.

But over time, silence gains weight. It presses on the chest. It teaches the body to hold breath instead of truth.

What began as survival slowly became a burden, one that shaped how you loved, trusted, and spoke.

Scripture

***Ecclesiastes 3:7(KJV)** "There is a time to be silent and a time to speak."*

Prayer

Lord, I stayed quiet because I did not know it was safe to speak. I learned to swallow pain instead of releasing it.

Teach me now that my voice is not a threat. That truth does not destroy what You are building.

That speaking does not mean I am ungrateful, disloyal, or weak.

Give me courage to exhale. To loosen what I have held inside for so long. To trust You with the sound of my truth.

Amen.

Chapter 5

Running Away and Learning How to Survive

At twelve years old, I ran away.

Grief, abuse, and silence made home unbearable. I ended up living with a friend on Montana Avenue in D.C., in the projects. For three months, hunger and hardship became my reality. Food stamps determined whether we ate.

But even there, I learned resilience.

The family took me in. I learned how to survive with very little. And I discovered strength I did not know I had.

Eventually, my cousin Bree found me and brought me home. Relief and fear collided. The world I had escaped still waited.

But I returned changed.

I had learned that I could endure. That God was guiding me even when I did not understand how.

And this was only the beginning.

Running away was not rebellion.

It was not recklessness.

It was instinct.

When staying meant being hurt again, leaving felt like the only way to live.

So I ran, not toward freedom, but toward air. Toward space. Toward distance from what threatened to break me.

Survival does not always look brave.

Sometimes it looks desperate.

Sometimes it looks like motion — any motion — just to stay alive.

Scripture

Psalm 18:17 (KJV) "He delivered me from my strong enemy… for they were too mighty for me."

Prayer

God, I did what I had to do to live. I ran because staying felt like dying inside.

You saw the nights I did not know where I belonged. You saw the choices I made just to make it to the next day. You did not abandon me, even when my life felt unstable.

Redeem what survival demanded of me. Heal the parts of my heart that learned to stay guarded. Teach me now how to live, not just endure.

Amen.

CHAPTER 6

Rebellion and the Need to Escape

Coming home didn't bring peace. My mother and I clashed constantly. Both grieving. Both hurting.

I rebelled—fighting, smoking, and escaping.

Yet I still prayed. Even broken prayers reach God.

These years shaped me—not to destroy me, but to prepare me.

CHAPTER 7

Motherhood and Independence

I was seventeen when I became a mother.

Holding my son Greg changed everything. I chose him when others told me not to. I left home to protect him.

By eighteen, I had two sons. Soon, three.

Motherhood taught me strength, faith, and fierce love.

Motherhood awakens something deep. It does not just bring life into the world; it brings memory.

Holding your child stirred the innocence I once carried. I saw in their eyes what should have been protected in mine. Their softness became both healing and grief, joy intertwined with mourning.

I did not just become a mother. I became a guardian of innocence, determined that the story would change here.

Scripture

> ***Psalm 127:3 (KJV)*** *"Children are a heritage from the Lord, offspring a reward from Him."*

Prayer

God,

When I became a mother, You trusted me with sacred ground. Tiny hearts. Tender spirits. Innocence still whole.

Heal the places in me that trembled with fear of repeating the past. Strengthen me where love felt overwhelming and responsibility felt heavy. Let my children receive what I did not: safety, voice, and protection.

Cover them where I cannot reach. Guard their innocence fiercely. And heal the child in me as I raise the children You have given me.

Amen.

Chapter 8

The Day I Set My Soul Free

Forgiveness changed my life.

I confronted my abuser. I forgave him. I forgave my mother. I forgave myself.

Forgiveness was not for them. It was for me.

That night, I slept free.

Freedom did not arrive loudly. There were no trumpets, no sudden erasing of memory.

It came quietly, in the moment I chose truth over hiding, release over resentment, and breath over silence.

Setting my soul free did not mean forgetting the past. It meant refusing to let it keep me bound.

Speaking my truth became worship. And silence no longer defined me.

Scripture

2 Corinthians 3:17 (KJV) "Now the Lord is the Spirit, and where the Spirit of the Lord is, there is freedom."

Prayer

Lord,

I release what has held me captive, not because it did not matter, but because it no longer gets to rule me.

I let go of shame that was never mine. I loosen the grip of fear that once kept me safe but now keeps me small. I choose freedom, even if it feels unfamiliar.

Teach my soul how to live unchained. Let healing continue its slow, holy work. And remind me that freedom is a journey You walk with me.

Amen.

CHAPTER 9

Struggle, Survival, and Seeds of Faith

Life remained hard, but faith began to grow.

My children anchored me. My father showed up in small but powerful ways.

Every prayer planted seeds.

Faith did not arrive when life was stable. It did not appear when questions were answered or wounds were healed.

Faith showed up quietly, in the middle of struggle, inside survival, planted like a seed in soil turned by pain.

I did not know how to pray yet. I did not have the language.

But something in me began to reach upward anyway.

That reaching mattered.

Scripture

Habakkuk 2:3 (KJV) *"Though it tarries, wait for it; because it will surely come."*

Prayer

God,

I did not come to You with certainty. I came with need. I brought questions, exhaustion, and a heart still learning how to trust.

Thank You for meeting me where I was, not where I thought I should be. For planting faith before I knew what to call it. For staying patient while belief took root slowly.

Water the seeds You planted. Strengthen what began in weakness. Let faith grow strong enough to withstand the storms ahead.

Amen.

CHAPTER 10

The Dream of Forgiveness

That night, I had a dream unlike any other, a dream that would change the way I saw forgiveness, myself, and the love of God.

I found myself standing in a long line among a multitude of people. These were not ordinary people. They did not have human bodies. Their forms were large, radiant, and angelic in appearance, tall and glowing, filled with light that seemed to pulse from within. As I looked closer, I saw something unusual in the center of their chests. It looked like a seed planted right in their hearts. Some had one, others three, others five.

When I looked down at myself, I saw four seeds glowing faintly inside my chest. I did not know what they were, but I could feel their weight. Later, God revealed to me that they were seeds of unforgiveness, the pain, anger, and guilt I had carried for so long and never released.

The moment He said that, memories flooded me, especially the one that had haunted me most.

I remembered the night I woke up and saw my brother, Lil' Greg, feeding his fish while waiting for a cab. I told him about a dream I had, how I had seen him die in a car accident. I begged him not to leave the house that night. He smiled and told me not to worry, that it was just a dream. He said he would be fine. But he left, and that was the last time I saw him. He died.

That memory pierced me. I could never forgive myself for not stopping him, for not finding a way to make him stay. I carried that pain for years, silently, deeply, endlessly.

As I stood in that long line, I began to hear something ahead. First came screams, agonizing and echoing, the cries of people in torment. Then came the sound of something slamming shut, an iron lid clanging, loud and final. It happened again and again, each time followed by cries that chilled my spirit.

The closer I moved to the front, the louder it became, until I could see what was ahead.

There was a great throne, beautiful and magnificent beyond description, but no one sat upon it. Only a powerful voice spoke, filling the air with authority and sorrow.

Before me stood a woman, trembling and weeping.

"Do you know why you are here?" the voice asked.

"Yes, Lord," she said through tears.

"This is what I have against you," He said, revealing the seeds in her chest. "You have led My people away from Me by what you have done on social media."

"But Lord, it is just social media!" she cried.

"You have caused My people to sin because of your nakedness," He said, quoting **Corinthians 6:19–20**. *"And for that, I am against you. Depart from Me."*

The iron door slammed shut, and her screams echoed as she was taken away. My body trembled. My spirit knew where she had gone.

Then it was my turn.

I fell to my knees, trembling uncontrollably, tears pouring from my eyes. "Lord, I do not know what I did, but please forgive me. Do not let me go to hell."

"My child, hear My voice," says the Lord.

"These are the ones you must forgive, and you must also forgive yourself. Search your heart and allow Me to reveal what still remains bound within you. Release it, and turn fully back to Me. Repent, and you will be made whole."

Then He told me to stand.

A screen appeared beside me, showing my entire life, every moment, every decision, every thought. A door opened, light poured through, and I heard, "You have been given permission to enter."

I stepped forward, and everything lifted.

I woke up crying, but free.

Forgiveness did not come as a command. It came as a glimpse. A dream. A moment of clarity.

A revelation that freedom might require release, even when the heart still ached.

This was not forgiveness fully formed. It was the idea of it. The seed planted before the work began.

God often introduces healing gently, not demanding obedience, but offering vision.

Scripture

Ephesians 4:32 (KJV) *"Be kind and compassionate to one another, forgiving each other, just as in Christ God forgave you."*

Prayer

Lord,

I did not know how to forgive. I only knew how to survive. But You showed me that forgiveness was not approval, and release was not denial.

I am not there yet, but I am willing to look. Willing to imagine freedom beyond resentment. Willing to trust that You would not ask this without grace.

Prepare my heart for the work ahead. Lead me gently, not ahead of healing, but alongside it.

Amen.

CHAPTER II

When Love Turns to Ashes

There are some chapters you never plan to write, not because the story is not real, but because the pain still burns when you touch it. This is one of those chapters.

Tye came into my life as a boy, but he became family. He was not born from my womb, yet he grew into my heart like a son. To my children, Rashad, Keshawn, and Greg, he was a brother. His bond with Keshawn was especially deep, instinctive, and protective.

Keshawn lived with Type 1 diabetes, and Tye carried that weight as if it were his own. He learned the warning signs before I ever had to explain them. When Keshawn's body faltered, Tye was already calling me or calling an ambulance. Fear lived in his eyes during those moments, the kind only love carries.

From the age of seven, Tye spent weekends and summers in my home. My house became his refuge. My children became his family.

Around the same time, my cousin Lotto reentered our lives. What began as visits slowly became something more permanent. Lotto was not just my cousin. He became my son in spirit. My home was his home.

"Cuz, I'm coming home," he would say.

And that is exactly what he meant.

He tried not to take up space. He cleaned to earn his keep. He stayed quiet, almost shrinking himself so I would not get tired of him being there. But I never was. I loved knowing he felt safe enough to rest.

Loss had already shaped these young men. Grief stitched them together. Love made them brothers.

Then came the night that shattered everything.

Lotto called me and asked if he could stay with Keshawn and my daughter, Ke'Shae. His father had put him out after quarantine. I told him yes. Of course I did. I explained that Keshawn was away celebrating his birthday, and I offered to call him.

"No, cuz," Lotto said. "Let him enjoy his birthday."

Even in rejection, Lotto thought of others.

Those were the last words I ever heard from him.

The next morning, a police officer called and told me someone had been murdered in the apartment.

The world stopped.

When I arrived, they told me Lotto was dead.

In that moment, something inside me broke open.

Shock turned into devastation. Devastation turned into betrayal. Somewhere in the chaos, I learned there was a warrant out for Tye's arrest. He was charged with first degree murder.

The grief that followed was unlike anything I had ever known. It was not just sorrow. It was confusion, horror, and heartbreak layered on top of heartbreak. I had opened my home to children who were not born to me and loved them as my own. Now that love stood in the ashes of tragedy.

We had no answers, only questions that screamed in the silence.

Grief came layered, sorrow, shock, betrayal, and confusion. We mourned Lotto deeply, painfully, and honestly. He was my cousin, my son in spirit, and a presence of love in our home. His life mattered. His loss shattered us.

And we grieved Tye too.

We mourned the boy who grew up in our home. The child we loved. The brother my children knew. Loss did not ask us to choose. It demanded that we carry both.

But my loyalty and love will always be for my cousin, Lotto.

There is no comparison.

That loyalty does not erase grief for Tye, nor does grief diminish love for Lotto. I will not rank sorrow or measure pain. I will not pretend love disappears when tragedy enters the room.

There were moments I blamed myself. If I had just said no. If I had closed my door this one time.

But the truth is, I never could have.

I loved them both too much.

And I still do.

This is what it means to be tried in the fire. Sometimes the flames do not come from enemies or strangers. They come from the ones you held closest. And all you can do is stand in the ashes, holding love, grief, and loyalty in the same trembling hands, trusting God with what no human heart can carry alone.

Scripture

Psalm 34:18 (KJV) *"The Lord is close to the brokenhearted and saves those who are crushed in spirit."*

This scripture speaks directly to the kind of grief in this chapter, the grief that comes from loss, betrayal, confusion, and unanswered questions. It reminds us that even when everything feels shattered, God draws nearer, not farther.

Prayer

Father God,

I come before You with a heart torn open. This pain is too heavy to carry alone, and only You can hold what we cannot.

You saw these boys when they were little, their laughter, their bond, their lives. You see the devastation left behind now.

I lift up the parents who lost both of their sons. There are no words for this kind of pain. Wrap them in Your arms when the silence is unbearable. Be their breath when grief steals the air from their lungs.

Lord, hold me and my children in this fire. Heal the wounds deeper than grief, the shock, the betrayal, and the unanswered questions. Protect our hearts from bitterness, our minds from memories that torment, and our souls from despair.

Jesus, You are acquainted with grief. Sit with us here. Teach us how to grieve without losing hope and how to mourn without losing our faith.

When answers never come, be the peace that remains. Hold every broken parent, including us, and remind us, even for a moment, that we are not alone.

In Jesus' name,

Amen.

CHAPTER 12

Reflection and Grace

Reflection taught me something powerful: I did the best I could with what I knew at the time.

For a long time, I carried guilt for the choices I made, the moments I wished I could redo, the reactions I regretted, and the decisions that felt heavy once I looked back at them. I judged myself harshly, believing that if I had known better, I would have done better. But reflection showed me the truth: I did do better, with the knowledge, strength, and tools I had at that moment.

Just like my mother did.

There were seasons in my life when I resented her for the choices she made. I did not understand why she handled things the way she did. I did not see her exhaustion, her fear, or the weight she carried as a young mother herself. All I saw was my pain. It was not until I became a mother that clarity came.

When I had children of my own, I found myself standing in similar places, making decisions without a rule book, choosing between imperfect options, loving fiercely while still learning as I went. In those moments, I realized something humbling: parenting does not come with instructions. It comes with love, mistakes, growth, and grace.

I saw myself in my mother.

I understood that she, too, was doing the best she could with what she knew at the time. She made choices based on survival, not selfishness. On protection, not neglect. On fear mixed with love, even when it did not look like love to me then.

That understanding softened my heart.

Reflection did not erase the pain of the past, but it reframed it. It allowed me to release bitterness and replace it with compassion. It taught me that grace is not pretending hurt did not happen. It is choosing not to let that hurt define the rest of my life.

Through reflection, I learned to extend grace to my mother, to myself, and to the generations before me. I learned that healing does not always come through answers, but through understanding. And understanding brings peace.

This chapter of my life was not about blame. It was about growth. It was about acknowledging that love can exist alongside mistakes, and that forgiveness does not mean forgetting, but freeing yourself.

Reflection gave me permission to breathe.

And in that breath, I found grace.

Reflection does not demand perfection. It invites honesty. It allows us to look back without condemnation and forward without fear. Grace does not deny pain. It simply refuses to let pain remain the narrator.

This chapter marks the moment when compassion replaced judgment, and understanding brought rest.

Scripture

Psalm 103:12 (KJV) *"As far as the east is from the west, so far has He removed our transgressions from us."*

Prayer

God,

Thank You for showing me that survival often looks like strength on the outside and fear on the inside. Thank You for teaching me compassion, not only for my mother, but for myself.

I release the burden of blame. I receive the gift of grace. And I choose healing over resentment, understanding over judgment, and peace over bitterness.

Amen.

CHAPTER 13

From Grief to Awakening

May 14, 2021 changed everything.

My father fell asleep behind the wheel of his SUV and ran into a metro bus in a head-on collision. He died instantly, and in that same moment, he was taken into the spiritual realm. That kind of pain felt like an elephant sitting on my chest, while at the same time being submerged underwater, suffocating for air. I was mentally and emotionally defeated. That morning, on my way home from the hospital, I tried to jump out of my husband's moving car. I had mentally left reality, but my husband saved me just in time.

Weeks later, Jesus answered my prayer in a dream, showing me my father healed, smiling, and alive in spirit. That dream brought a peace I had never known. The Lord Jesus allowed me to speak to my dad as he smiled and listened. He never said a word, but he nodded his head yes when I said, "Dad, you're okay." I placed my hands on his chest. It was wrapped in white bandages, covering the wounded area that caused his death.

It was the beginning of my spiritual awakening.

Grief has a way of stripping life down to its core.

It removes distractions. It silences noise. It leaves only questions and longing.

Losing my father did not just break my heart. It awakened a deeper hunger to understand what lies beyond this life. Although I wished I had been in that SUV that morning to save my father's life, I knew I was powerless. Yet in that moment, for the first time in my life, I felt the Heavenly Father's love in the most profound way. It rained down on me from heaven.

I understood how deeply the Father loved His beloved Son, Jesus. I understood that He could have destroyed the whole earth to save Him, yet He did nothing. He had to sit back and watch His Son be beaten and crucified by His own creation. In that moment, I felt His unconditional love, grace, and mercy for me. He loves you and me so much that He sent His only begotten Son to save you and me.

My spirit instantly felt both the love and the sorrow of my Heavenly Father. All I could do was weep for hours, feeling both my sorrow and the sorrow of my loving and merciful Father.

The dream was not coincidence.

It was comfort.

It was God answering sorrow with revelation instead of explanation.

In the middle of loss, Jesus showed me that love does not end with death. It transforms.

Scripture

John 11:25 (KJV) "I am the resurrection and the life. The one who believes in Me will live, even though they die."

Prayer

Jesus,

I did not know how to carry the weight of losing my father. My heart was heavy, my questions unanswered, my grief deep. But You met me gently.

You showed me peace when I needed it most. You revealed that death does not have the final word. Thank You for awakening my spirit through sorrow. Thank You for reminding me that heaven is real and love continues.

Lead me into what this awakening is preparing me for.

Amen.

CHAPTER 14

Healing, Forgiveness, and Restoration

After my father's passing, something shifted in me. I forgave my abuser. I forgave my mother. I forgave myself.

Healing did not come all at once, but it came. God restored what trauma tried to destroy.

Forgiveness did not come from pressure. It came from clarity.

Something softened after grief.

Something loosened after awakening.

The grip of the past weakened, not because it did not matter, but because it no longer had authority.

Forgiveness was not agreement with what happened. It was release from carrying it any longer. And healing followed, slowly, gently, honestly.

Scripture

Psalm 147:3 (KJV) *"He heals the brokenhearted and binds up their wounds."*

Prayer

God,

Thank You for the courage to forgive what once felt unforgivable. Thank You for meeting me at my pace, not forcing healing before I was ready.

I receive the restoration You promised. You restore my joy. You restore my peace. You restore the parts of me trauma tried to silence. Let what was broken become whole again, not erased, but redeemed.

Amen.

CHAPTER 15

Trials and Divine Protection

Life has a way of testing your faith, your courage, and your heart. Just when I thought we had overcome the worst, another storm came knocking at our door.

Keshawn, my second son, had already battled diabetes, and his life had been hanging by a thread. Then, one June morning in 2023, his glucose levels skyrocketed to 509. He went into diabetic ketoacidosis (DKA) and was rushed to the hospital. For two long weeks, I prayed, fasted, and played gospel music at his bedside. I begged God to preserve his life. Every moment felt like a lifetime. But by the grace of Jesus, his kidneys were fine. The doctors called it a miracle — but I knew it was divine intervention.

Just when I thought we could breathe, danger came again. His baby mother, Naya, returned — this time with her brother, her boyfriend, and two girls — all armed and dangerous, intent on harming Keshawn. As they approached, Rashad, my brave and protective son, intervened. Shots rang out. One bullet flew dangerously close to Rashad — it missed him, but the fear of losing him shook me to my core.

Keshawn, weak from his recent illness, fought to protect himself and his family. I remember thinking, *Lord, not again. Please protect my children.*

I wasn't there when it started — the chaos unfolded through frantic calls from both Keshawn and Rashad. My heart raced as I rushed to the scene. When I arrived, I spoke firmly with the detective assigned to the case. At first, he believed Keshawn was guilty and Rashad the victim. I told him the truth — that Keshawn was also a victim — and pointed to the security cameras. I insisted everyone involved be detained before my sons came forward.

Despite everything, Keshawn was arrested and charged with first-degree assault and attempted murder. Seeing my son locked up — unable to receive insulin — broke me. But I refused to be silent. I hired an attorney and stood firm.

Two weeks later, every charge was dropped. His record was cleared. He came home alive. I knew then — God's protection is real.

Some trials feel unbearable not because they are new — but because they come after you thought the danger had passed.

You had already prayed.

Already fasted.

Already watched God move once. And still — another storm rose.

This chapter is proof that faith is not the absence of fear, but the refusal to surrender when fear shows up again.

Scripture

Psalm 34:7 (KJV) *"The angel of the Lord encamps around those who fear Him, and He delivers them."*

Prayer

God,

You saw what tried to take my sons. You stood between bullets, illness, injustice, and loss.

Thank You for the protection I could see and the protection I never knew about. Thank You for defending my children when systems failed and danger surrounded them.

I place my sons under Your covering again. Guard their bodies, their minds, and their futures.

Let no weapon formed against them prosper. Amen.

CHAPTER 16

The Visitation

That night, everything changed.

Taj and I were lying in bed. I wasn't asleep — my eyes were open. Suddenly, I felt something powerful sweep through the room. In an instant, it was as if my soul was lifted from my body. I could see myself lying there, and fear rushed over me.

I cried out to God, asking forgiveness for every doubt, every failure, every moment I turned away.

Then I heard His voice — not loud, but filled with peace and authority. **He spoke the words of Jeremiah 29:11:**

"For I know the plans I have for you," declares the Lord, "plans to prosper you and not to harm you, plans to give you hope and a future."

Peace flooded my spirit. I knew God was not finished with me.

When I returned fully to myself, Taj was holding my hand. He knew something holy had happened. From that moment on, I was changed. Fear was replaced with peace. Purpose became clear.

It wasn't just a vision.

It was a visitation.

Some encounters don't come with explanations — they come with assurance. In one moment, fear rises. In the next, heaven speaks.

God did not meet you with condemnation. He met you with promise.

And the promise wasn't vague — it was personal: hope, future, purpose.

This chapter is a turning point because it marks the moment you realized: you were never forgotten — you were being called.

Scripture

> ***2 Timothy 1:7(KJV)*** *"For God has not given us a spirit of fear, but of power and of love and of a sound mind."*

Prayer

Lord,

Thank You for meeting me in a moment I could not control. Thank You for speaking peace where fear tried to rule.

I receive Your promise. I release every lie that says I am finished, forgotten, or disqualified.

Anchor me in purpose. Strengthen me in faith. And keep my spirit sensitive to Your voice.

Amen.

CHAPTER 17

The Dream of the Man in White

That Night, I Dreamed

That night, I dreamed a dream unlike any other.

I heard three gentle knocks at the door. When I opened it, a man stood there wearing a pure white suit, glowing with light. His hair was white as snow. His presence calmed everything around us.

He asked, "May I come in?"

I said yes.

Inside, we sat at a table. Before him was a large book. He turned its pages slowly, teaching me. His lips moved, but the words are gone now — only the peace remains.

Before leaving, he said, *"Keep walking in faith. Your story is unfolding exactly as it should."*

When I woke, **Revelation 3:20** came to mind:

"Behold, I stand at the door and knock..."

I knew then — God was guiding me gently, step by step.

Scriptures

Revelation 3:20 (KJV) *"Behold, I stand at the door, and knock: if any man hear my voice, and open the door, I will come in to him, and will sup with him, and he with me."*

Daniel 7:9 (KJV) *"I beheld till the thrones were cast down, and the Ancient of days did sit, whose garment was white as snow, and the hair of his head like the pure wool..."*

Prayer

Father God,

Thank You for being near — so near that You knock. Thank You for the kind of presence that doesn't force the door, but waits with love until I say yes.

Lord Jesus, I open my heart again to You.

Come in and sit with me. Teach me even when I can't remember every word, and let Your peace be the proof that You were here.

If my mind forgets the details, let my spirit hold the truth: You are guiding me — gently, faithfully, step by step.

God, as You turn the pages of my life, help me trust what You are writing. When I feel unsure of what's next, remind me that my story is unfolding exactly as it should.

Give me strength to keep walking in faith, even when I can't see far ahead. Let my home be a place where Your presence is welcomed. Let my table be a place of communion with You. And let my life be a living "yes" to the One who stands at the door and knocks.

I receive Your peace.

I receive Your direction.

I receive Your presence.

In Jesus' name,

Amen.

Chapter 18

Living Fully, Loving Deeply

Living with Intention

Now, I live with intention. Every day is a gift. I love deeply, laugh freely, and walk in gratitude. My past no longer defines me — it prepared me.

Even when challenges arise, I face them with courage, knowing God equipped me through every storm. I am living proof.

God did not rush in.

He knocked.

He asked permission — not because He lacked authority, but because He honors relationship. Your yes mattered.

The peace you felt was not accidental. Peace is often the confirmation of His presence. Some encounters are not meant to be fully remembered — they are meant to be felt, trusted, and followed.

Scripture

Revelation 3:20 (KJV) *"Behold, I stand at the door and knock. If anyone hears my voice and opens the door, I will come in."*

This verse reminds us that God leads with invitation, not force. He waits for our response.

Prayer

Lord,

Thank You for knocking gently. Thank You for meeting me with peace instead of fear. Help me continue to say yes — even when I don't understand every step.

Guide me as You unfold my story, page by page.

Amen.

Chapter 19

Healing and Reflecting

Healing is a Journey

Healing is not a straight path. Some days, memories of past pain resurface like waves crashing against the shore. But I've learned that acknowledging the pain, rather than burying it, allows true healing to take place.

I journal my thoughts, pray for clarity, and lean on faith as my constant anchor. Reflection has become a powerful tool — a way to understand not just what I've endured, but how I've grown. Each challenge I faced has shaped my character, strengthened my resolve, and deepened my empathy for others.

I also take time to celebrate victories — both big and small. Overcoming a fear, speaking my truth, nurturing my family, and finding joy in simple moments — these are milestones of healing that deserve recognition. Healing is active. It requires persistence, honesty, and self-love.

Healing does not ask us to forget. It asks us to face, feel, and honor what we have survived. Reflection becomes your mirror — not to relive pain, but to witness growth.

By acknowledging the waves instead of fighting them, you learn how to stay standing in the water.

Scripture

Psalm 147:3 (KJV) *"He heals the brokenhearted and binds up their wounds."*

Healing is not rushed. It is intentional, patient, and deeply personal.

Prayer

God,

Thank You for walking with me through every layer of healing. Thank You for meeting me in honesty instead of perfection.

Help me remain patient with myself. Teach me to honor progress — even when it feels small.

Let reflection continue to bring clarity, strength, and peace.

Amen.

CHAPTER 20

Freedom, Family, and Purpose

Living in Gratitude and Purpose

Today, I live a life I once could only dream of — a life filled with love, faith, and purpose. Every morning, I wake with gratitude in my heart: for my husband Taj, for my children, for my grandchildren, and for the journey that brought me here.

Every scar, every tear, every trial I endured has been a step toward this life. A life where I can breathe freely, love fully, and walk boldly in my purpose. I look back on the storms of the past — the trials that seemed unbearable — and I see how each one strengthened me, sharpened my faith, and deepened my reliance on God.

Family is my anchor. My siblings — Mia, Monique, Marie, Montae, Dave Jermaine, and Dre — have been pillars in my life. I remember my brothers who passed too soon, Lil Greg and Jermaine. I honor their memory every day. The love of my parents, my mother Nina and my father Gregory Sr., remains a guiding light, reminding me that no matter the obstacles, family is the foundation that holds us steady.

Through every battle, my faith has been my shield. I have witnessed miracles, protection in times of danger, and divine guidance that has carried me through moments when hope seemed distant. I have learned that freedom is not just the absence of struggle — it is the peace and confidence that come from knowing God is with you.

Purpose is what drives me forward. I know now that my life is not my own — it is a testament to endurance, faith, and the power of God's love. Sharing my story is part of that purpose. I want others who feel broken, lost, or overwhelmed to know that there is hope, that there is healing, and that there is a path to freedom if you hold on and trust in God's plan.

As I embrace each day, I celebrate life, love, and faith. I celebrate the lessons learned and the victories won. And I rejoice in the knowledge that the journey continues, guided by grace, anchored in family, and fueled by purpose.

Life is a gift. Every breath, every heartbeat, every smile is a reminder of God's goodness. I am living proof that even after the fiercest storms, we can rise, shine, and walk in the fullness of our calling.

Freedom is not forgetting the storm. It is standing after it. Your life now speaks where words once failed.

What you endured became evidence.

What you survived became purpose.

This chapter does not end the journey — it blesses the road ahead.

Scripture

Psalm 126:3 (KJV) *"The Lord has done great things for us, and we are filled with joy."*

This is gratitude that comes from experience — not theory, not ease, but faithfulness.

Prayer

God,

Thank You for carrying me through every season. Thank You for family, faith, and freedom.

Use my life as a light for others. Let my story remind the broken that healing is possible and purpose is real.

I walk forward with gratitude, courage, and trust.

Amen.

CHAPTER 21

The Day the Mirror Didn't Smile

The Mirror of Becoming

The night carried a strange heaviness, the kind that settles deep in the chest without asking permission. I lay down only to rest, but what met me was something far deeper — a dream that felt like revelation.

In the dream, I stood alone in a dimly lit room. No sound. No movement. Just me... and a mirror.

At first, I didn't think anything of it. I had looked in mirrors a thousand times before. But this time, something felt different. The mirror seemed to breathe, almost waiting for me to come closer.

So I stepped forward.

And then — I froze.

Because the face staring back at me... didn't smile. It was me. And yet, it wasn't the me I thought I knew.

But the dream didn't end there.

As I leaned in closer, the mirror shifted — almost like it rippled — and another image formed right beside my reflection. This time, it was her. The older me.

This was not a dream of vanity — it was a vision of becoming.

God did not show me who I was failing to be. He showed me who I was growing into. The older version of me carried peace, not perfection. She carried wisdom earned through fire.

Sometimes God lets us see the end so we don't give up in the middle.

She didn't frighten me. She didn't judge me. She simply existed, calm and steady, with long white hair flowing down like strands of moonlight. Her eyes held something mine didn't yet — the quiet knowing that comes from surviving storms.

And without words, she looked at me as if to say:

"You made it. You survive. You endure. And you become me."

Standing there — caught between who I was and who I would become — I felt the furnace all over again. But this time, I realized:

The fire wasn't meant to burn me. It was meant to refine me.

The mirror wasn't judging me. It was revealing me.

My reflection wasn't my enemy. It was my evolution.

For the first time, I didn't turn away. I faced both versions of myself, the now and the not-yet, and accepted that both belonged to me.

Because this is what the furnace does: It removes what is temporary, so the eternal can be seen.

Scripture

2 Corinthians 3:18 (KJV) *"And we all, who with unveiled faces contemplate the Lord's glory, are being transformed into His image."*

Transformation is not sudden. It is revealed in layers.

Prayer

God,

Thank You for showing me who I am becoming. Thank You for reminding me that the fire refines — it does not destroy.

Help me honor the process. Help me stay present in the becoming. And help me trust that what You are forming in me is eternal.

Amen.

CHAPTER 22

A Dream of the Narrow Way

The Narrow Way

In a dream, the Lord led me to a great house — new, clean, and already owned, yet open to me. I felt no fear, only peace.

I entered through a door where the stairs were narrow and rising high. As I climbed, I heard a voice say, "Only a certain kind of body can pass here."

And I understood — not strength, not pride, but humility and surrender make room to ascend. Each step lifted me higher, lighter than before.

My family was there — those still living and those resting with the Lord — together, whole, and joyful. We lived close, like connected homes, separate yet bound by love. There was no confusion, only belonging. No loss, only continuity.

And the Lord showed me: this was not a dream of distance, but of inheritance — a calling to rise while remaining rooted, to walk the narrow way into the home He prepared.

This dream was not about achievement. It was about alignment.

The stairs were narrow because ego cannot climb them. Fear cannot pass through them. Only surrender fits.

What you were shown was not exclusion — it was invitation. An inheritance already prepared. A home already owned. A path that requires humility, not performance.

Scripture

Matthew" 7:13–14 (KJV) through the narrow gate… small is the gate and narrow the road that leads to life."

The narrow way is not harsh. It is precise.

It leads to life, belonging, and peace.

Prayer

Lord,

Thank You for showing me that the way upward is the way inward. Strip me of what cannot follow You.

Clothe me in humility, obedience, and trust. Help me walk the narrow way with joy — not striving, not fear, but surrender.

Thank You for the inheritance You prepared long before I arrived.

Amen.

CHAPTER 23

The House, the Glowing Wood, and the Keys

The Dream of Stewardship

I had a dream one night that stayed with me long after I woke. In it, I was invited into the home of a man who followed Christ. He welcomed me and a group of other followers, showing us wood I had never seen before.

It was fine, glowing wood — unlike anything I had ever touched or imagined.

He spoke passionately about a plan to flee to the New Jerusalem, a place of safety, hope, and eternal alignment with God's promises. The glow of the wood captivated me. I felt it symbolized something precious — something refined. It felt alive with purpose, as though each grain had been carefully shaped, polished by fire.

In that moment, I realized God was showing me the beauty of faith refined through trials. The furnace of life, though painful, produces something lasting, something that shines even when darkness surrounds it.

But suddenly, the peace of the house was shattered. The police kicked down the door and arrested the man of God. I watched in shock as he was taken away, his voice silenced, his presence removed.

Immediately after, another man came into the house, declaring that he would take over. Everything shifted. The warmth and glow of the space felt threatened, replaced with tension and unease. I knew instinctively that not everyone who steps into leadership carries God's Spirit.

After the man of God was arrested, I took his keys and his phone. In dreams, these objects carry weight. Keys are a symbol of stewardship, access, and responsibility. Phones represent communication, connection, and the continuation of a message.

God was showing me that even when leaders are removed, faithful witnesses are entrusted with preserving truth, continuing testimony, and guarding what cannot be taken away. It was not about seizing control, but about responsibility — about trustworthiness.

In reflection, the dream felt like a mirror of life itself.

- The glowing wood reminded me that God is always refining our faith through trials.

- The plan to flee to the New Jerusalem symbolized hope — the ultimate promise of God's eternal kingdom.

- The arrest and takeover reminded me that truth will always face opposition, but God's purposes cannot be thwarted.

- And the keys and the phone revealed my role: to be faithful, discerning, and protective of the message God has placed in my hands.

God was showing me that my calling is not to chase authority or control, but to preserve the faith, the message, and the testimony He has entrusted to me.

Even when leadership fails.

Even when opposition comes.

Even when the world seems chaotic.

The work God has begun cannot be taken.

This dream was a reminder that the furnace of life, no matter how hot, is not meant to destroy. It is meant to refine. It is meant to prepare us to carry God's truth with wisdom, courage, and faithfulness.

Even when the fire rages, even when doors are broken down, and even when voices are silenced — God's truth endures. And those willing to be faithful stewards will always be entrusted with what matters most.

This dream was not symbolic curiosity. It was spiritual instruction. God was not merely showing me what happens when leaders fall. He was showing me who He trusts when they do.

The house represents spiritual dwelling — a place where truth lives.

The glowing wood represents faith refined by fire — not manufactured, not polished by appearance, but tested, enduring, alive.

And the keys? The keys are not power. They are permission. God does not give keys to the loudest voice. He gives keys to the faithful witness.

This was heaven saying:

"What I entrusted to one, I now entrust to another — not for control, but for custody."

I was shown that truth survives disruption, and calling outlives position.

Scripture

2 Timothy 2:2 (KJV) — *"What you have heard from me... entrust to faithful people who will be able to teach others also."*

Prayer

God,

You refined me so You could trust me. You tested me so You could entrust me. Keep my hands clean.

Keep my heart humble. Keep my discernment sharp.

Let me never confuse stewardship with control or calling with pride. I will guard what You give.

I will speak what You say. I will remain faithful — even when the fire returns.

Amen.

Chapter 24

When Death Spoke, God Answered

The diagnosis came like a verdict that could not be appealed.

Stage 4 T-Cell Lymphoma. Aggressive. Advanced. Terminal.

The doctors spoke carefully, but the meaning was unmistakable. My husband, Taj, was facing a cancer that, by every medical standard, was already supposed to have won. Treatment began immediately, and with it came hope. Not the kind rooted in certainty, but the kind that clings simply because it has no other choice.

One chemotherapy treatment failed.

Then another.

Then another.

Then another.

Then another.

Five different chemotherapy regimens. None of them worked.

Each treatment weakened his body, but the cancer remained unmoved. His strength faded. His weight dropped. His eyes carried exhaustion that words could not hold. Hope became something we chose minute by minute, breath by breath. And when medicine reached its limit, I went to God.

I fasted.

I prayed.

I cried out, not eloquently, not calmly, but desperately.

One night, God answered.

In a dream, I saw my husband's body, but it was not as I knew it. There was no skin, only a skeletal frame, fragile, exposed, stripped down to what cancer had tried to leave behind. It was a sight that should have terrified me, but before fear could take root, I saw the hand of God.

It covered his chest.

Not his entire body.

Not the disease.

His chest, where his heart and lungs lived, where breath still mattered.

Then the dream shifted.

I saw Johns Hopkins Hospital.

Clear. Distinct. Unmistakable.

I woke up knowing this was not imagination. It was not symbolism meant to confuse. It was instruction.

Two months later, with no improvement and no new options offered, I contacted Johns Hopkins Cancer Treatment Center. At the time, there was no guarantee they could help. No promise. No assurance that this would change anything.

Only obedience.

One month later, Taj was accepted into treatment there.

And something changed.

Where cancer had resisted everything before, it began to retreat. Where death had spoken confidently, it suddenly went quiet. Slowly, impossibly, the disease that had ignored five treatments began to lose ground.

Then came the words we had not dared to expect.

Remission.

Time passed.

Not weeks.

Not months.

Years.

Scan after scan showed the same impossible result. No evidence of disease.

Three years later, doctors continued to report no signs of cancer anywhere in his system. They reviewed records. They questioned timelines. They were confused, because this cancer, by every medical definition, was terminal.

Yet my husband was standing.

Breathing.

Living.

What medicine could not explain, heaven had already answered.

God showed me that when the body is reduced to nothing, His hand is still enough. The dream was never about death. It was about authority. Cancer touched what it could, but God covered what mattered. The furnace burned hot, but it did not destroy. It refined. It revealed. It prepared us to witness what only God could do.

The diagnosis said terminal.

The treatments said failure.

But God said covered.

And His word was final.

CHAPTER 25

After the Miracle

Miracles do not end the story. They change the way you live inside it.

After the words "no evidence of disease" were spoken, life did not suddenly become perfect. There were no trumpets, no instant return to normal, no forgetting what we had walked through. What came instead was something quieter — and heavier.

Stewardship.

We learned that surviving a miracle requires just as much faith as believing for one. The fear did not vanish overnight. Every ache raised questions. Every appointment carried memory. But each clear scan became a reminder that what God had done was not temporary.

It was sustained.

Three years passed. Then more. And every report came back the same: no signs of cancer. No trace. No explanation. Doctors grew careful with their words, choosing observation over certainty because the outcome did not match the diagnosis they once gave.

What they called confusion, we called confirmation.

God had not only healed — He had kept.

After the miracle, my faith matured. It no longer asked God to prove Himself. It learned how to trust Him without needing constant reassurance. Prayer became less frantic and more anchored. Gratitude replaced panic. Worship replaced pleading.

I also learned that miracles do not erase memory — they redeem it.

The nights of fear did not disappear, but they no longer held authority. The hospital rooms that once echoed with uncertainty now testified of God's faithfulness. Even the word terminal lost its grip because we had seen how temporary human conclusions are in the presence of divine will.

After the miracle, my marriage deepened. We no longer loved from survival alone, but from reverence — aware that life is not promised, but entrusted. Every ordinary day became sacred. Every laugh carried weight. Every breath felt borrowed and blessed at the same time.

God taught me that miracles are not rewards for the strong.

They are revelations for the surrendered.

He also taught me that healing is not just physical. It is emotional. Spiritual. Generational. What cancer tried to take from our future, God restored with purpose. What fear tried to steal from our peace, God replaced with confidence.

After the miracle, I stopped asking "Why us?" and started asking, "How can this serve?" I understood that testimony is not meant to be stored — it is meant to be shared. Someone else's faith may be waiting on the courage it takes to speak what God has done.

We did not return to who we were before the diagnosis.

We became who the furnace prepared us to be.

Still believing.

Still praying.

Still trusting.

But now, with evidence.

Because after the miracle, faith is no longer theoretical. It is lived.

I once believed the fire came to end me. I understand now — it came to reveal me.

The furnace stripped away what could not survive pressure: fear that ruled my choices, silence that kept me bound, strength that depended on control instead of trust. What remained was faith refined enough to breathe in heat, hope that did not collapse under delay, and a love anchored beyond circumstance.

I did not walk through the fire untouched. I walked through it changed.

The furnace did not make me perfect. It made me faithful.

Every trial carried purpose, even when I could not see it. Every loss shaped endurance. Every unanswered prayer taught me how to wait without breaking. The fire did not take my life — it prepared it.

If you are reading this while still standing in the heat — still praying, still believing, still holding on — know this: the furnace is not proof that God has abandoned you. It is evidence that He is at work.

What burns away was never meant to remain. What survives will carry you forward.

I move on now — not because the journey was easy, but because God was faithful through it all. And I know this to be true: The fire did not win. It refined.

Scripture Index

Tried in the Furnace: My Journey from Pain to Purpose

Isaiah 43:2 — Chapter 1, Innocence Interrupted

Psalm 34:18 — Chapters 2 and 11

Psalm 56:8 — Chapter 3

Ecclesiastes 3:7 — Chapter 4

Psalm 18:17 — Chapter 5

Psalm 127:3 — Chapter 7

2 Corinthians 3:17 — Chapter 8

Habakkuk 2:3 — Chapter 9

Ephesians 4:32 — Chapter 10

Psalm 103:12 — Chapter 12

John 11:25 — Chapter 13

Psalm 147:3 — Chapters 14 and 19

Psalm 34:7 — Chapter 15

2 Timothy 1:7 — Chapter 16

Revelation 3:20 — Chapters 17 and 18

Daniel 7:9 — Chapter 17

Psalm 126:3 — Chapter 20

2 Corinthians 3:18 — Chapter 21

Matthew 7:13–14 — Chapter 22

2 Timothy 2:2 — Chapter 23

A Blessing From My Heart to Yours

If you are holding this book with tired hands, if you've read these pages through tears, questions, or quiet endurance,

I want you to know something first:

You are not weak for what you've survived.

You are not abandoned because the fire hasn't ended yet.

I've stood where you stand.

I've prayed prayers that felt unanswered.

I've waited longer than I thought my heart could endure.

And I've learned this — God does not leave us in the furnace alone.

And neither did Jesus escape it.

Before there was resurrection, there was tribulation.

Before healing flowed, there were wounds.

Before forgiveness reached the world, there was a cross.

Jesus went through the fire Himself.

He was rejected.

He was beaten.

He was misunderstood.

He was crucified.

And from that suffering was born salvation for the whole world.

His pain gave birth to forgiveness.

His surrender took the keys from death and the grave.

His wounds released healing.

His suffering became the most powerful testimony the world has ever known.

So if you ever find yourself wanting to blame Jesus for the furnace you're in, remember — He entered it first.

Not to harm you.

But to redeem you.

Because the truth is this:

The most powerful testimony used to heal others is almost always born from pain and suffering.

That doesn't mean God delights in your hurt.

It means He refuses to waste it.

My prayer for you is simple and sincere:

May you find strength on the days you feel empty.

May peace meet you when fear tries to speak louder than hope.

May Jesus remind you — again and again — that your story is not over.

If the fire is hot right now, please hear me:

It is not here to destroy you.

It is shaping something in you that will bring life to others.

I pray that what you've lost does not define you, and what you've endured does not harden you.

May your heart stay open.

May your faith keep breathing — even when it feels fragile.

And when you come through this season — and you will —

I pray you look back and see not just pain, but purpose.

Not just survival, but redemption.

From one who has walked through the fire to another still standing in it, may you walk forward refined, held, and deeply loved.

And may you always remember this:

Jesus went through the fire too.

And the fire did not win.

About the Author

Keisha Sheppard is a wife, mother, grandmother, and survivor whose life stands as a testimony to the power of faith, forgiveness, and perseverance. Born and raised in Washington, D.C., she has endured childhood trauma, profound loss, grief, and seasons of hardship that could have silenced her voice—but instead refined her purpose.

Through every trial, Keisha discovered that pain does not have the final word. Anchored in her faith in Jesus Christ, she learned that healing is possible, forgiveness is freeing, and restoration can rise from even the deepest wounds. Her journey has been marked by divine encounters, spiritual awakening, and an unshakable belief that God wastes nothing—not even suffering.

Tried in the Furnace: My Journey from Pain to Purpose is her testimony. Written not to expose, but to heal; not to condemn, but to restore, Keisha shares her story so that others who feel broken, overwhelmed, or forgotten may know they are seen, loved, and never beyond redemption.

Today, Keisha lives with intention and gratitude, devoted to her family and committed to walking boldly in her God-given purpose. Through her story, she reminds readers that the fire meant to destroy can become the place where faith is forged—and that with God, survival can become transformation.

Back Cover Description

What happens when life places you in the fire—and walking away is not an option?

Tried in the Furnace: My Journey from Pain to Purpose is a raw, faith-filled testimony of survival, suffering, and sacred transformation. Through trauma, loss, betrayal, illness, and moments when hope felt out of reach, Keisha Sheppard takes readers on a journey where pain does not have the final word.

This book is not about a life without trials. It is about a God who meets us in them. From childhood wounds and generational brokenness to motherhood, forgiveness, spiritual awakening, and miraculous healing, *Tried in the Furnace* shows how the fire that threatens to destroy can instead refine, reveal, and prepare us for purpose.

Through dreams, prayer, fasting, and unwavering faith, Keisha testifies to a God who still heals, still speaks, and still carries His people through impossible circumstances—including a terminal cancer diagnosis that ended in remission against all odds.

Written for anyone who has ever asked, "Why me?" this book offers reassurance, hope, and truth:

You are not abandoned.

You are not forgotten.

The fire is not the end of your story.

If you are in the furnace right now—waiting, hurting, believing—this testimony will remind you that Jesus went through the fire too, and because He did, you do not walk alone.

If He carried me through the fire, He will carry you too.

My Journey from Pain to Purpose

www.ingramcontent.com/pod-product-compliance
Lightning Source LLC
Chambersburg PA
CBHW020333010526
44119CB00002B/48